CONTENTS

	PAGE
The Spooky Skaters: The Graffiti Ghost	**4–40**
People and places	**4–5**
The Spooky Skaters: The Graffiti Ghost	**6–31**
Fact Files	**32–37**
Graffiti: Art from the street!	**32–33**
Art galleries: Three of the best!	**34–35**
Pablo Picasso	**36–37**
Self-Study Activities	**38–40**
New Words	**inside back cover**

Material written by: Angela Salt

Illustrator: Stuart Harrison

Publisher: Jacquie Bloese

Editor: Emma Grisewood

Designer: Mo Choy

Picture Research: Pupak Navabpour

Photo credits:
Pages 32 & 33: G Rancinan, J Donoso/Corbis;
D Etheridge-Barnes/Getty Images; A Gallery/Alamy.
Pages 34 & 35: R Rivas/AFP/GettyImages; R Roberts,
D Delimont, croftsphoto/Alamy.
Pages 36 & 37: Succession Picasso/DACS 2008;
Photos12.com/Oronoz; Philadelphia Museum of Art/Corbis.
SPOOKY SKATERS™ & © Fun Crew Ltd.
© Fun Crew Ltd. 2009

Published by Scholastic Ltd 2009

Mary Glasgow Magazines (Scholastic Ltd.)
Euston House
24 Eversholt Street
London
NW1 1DB

Printed in Singapore

ADAM, RICK AND MIA ARE THREE FRIENDS. THEY LIVE IN A BIG CITY. THEY LOVE SKATING AND GRAFFITI ART!

PABLO IS A DEAD SPANISH PAINTER – WITH PROBLEMS! HE LIVES IN THE LAND OF THE DEAD.

PLACES

THE LAND OF THE DEAD IS UNDER THE LAND OF THE LIVING. THE SPOOKY SKATERS LIVE THERE. THEY THINK IT'S BORING. AT NIGHT, THEY GO UP TO THE LAND OF THE LIVING IN THEIR HALF-PIPE.

THE SUBWAY IS A GREAT PLACE TO SKATE. ADAM, RICK AND MIA MEET HERE. IT IS NEXT TO A BIG ART GALLERY.

DURING THE HOLIDAYS, ADAM, RICK AND MIA LIKED TO SKATE TOGETHER. THEIR FAVOURITE HANG-OUT WAS A SUBWAY UNDER THE CITY ART GALLERY.

IT'S GREAT SKATING HERE! IT'S A BREAK FROM HOMEWORK.

RICK ENJOYS A BREAK! LOOK AT HIS ARM!

IT WAS A VERY DIFFICULT STUNT!

YEAH! SORRY I DIDN'T HAVE MY CAMERA, THAT DAY!

CRACK!

LET'S START OUR MURAL. CAN YOU STILL HELP, RICK?

NO PROBLEM. I'M LEFT-HANDED. LET'S PAINT!

* Every town and city in the UK has a council. The council runs the town.

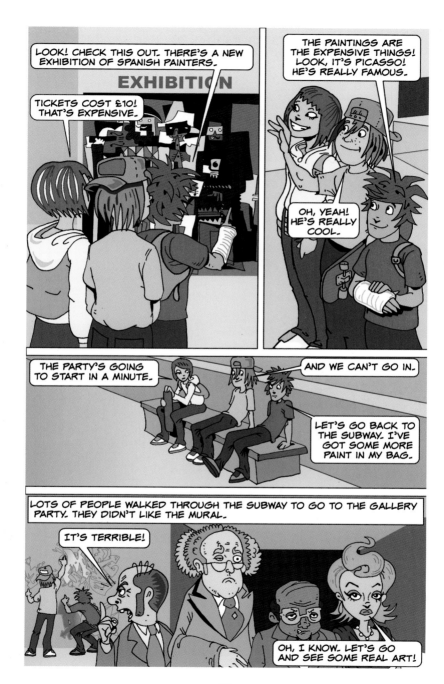

FAR AWAY IN THE LAND OF THE DEAD, THE SPOOKY SKATERS - RIP, JINX, HEX, ZOMBOY AND JUJU - WERE BORED.

LISTEN TO THAT RAIN!

WE CAN'T SKATE IN THIS BAD WEATHER.

IT'S BORING DOWN HERE.

I KNOW! LET'S PAINT OUR ROOM! WE NEED NEW COLOURS.

YUK! YELLOW WALLS?

NOT PINK! I HATE PINK!

PARP!

I DON'T CARE! I'M GOING TO PABLO'S PAINT SHOP. SEE YOU LATER!

THE BORED BOYS WENT UP TO THE LAND OF THE LIVING TO SKATE. AT NIGHT THEIR HALF-PIPE COMES UP THROUGH THE GROUND ...

WHERE ARE WE, RIP?

RUMBLE!

I DON'T KNOW. MAYBE THAT BUILDING'S AN ART GALLERY. THERE ARE LOTS OF PEOPLE ABOUT.

ARGHH! WE CAN'T SKATE WITH THEM HERE!

HEY - I CAN HEAR MUSIC. LET'S CHECK IT OUT.

OK, BUT BE CAREFUL! NO-ONE MUST SEE US.

ADAM, RICK AND MIA LEFT THE SUBWAY. IT WAS DARK BUT MIA SAW SOMEONE ...

HEY! THE PAINT'S STILL WET! BE CAREFUL!

THE NEXT EVENING, IN THE LAND OF THE LIVING, ADAM, RICK AND MIA MET IN THE SUBWAY.

HI!

TODAY WAS THE WORST DAY OF MY LIFE.

DID YOU SEE THE T.V. LAST NIGHT? THAT PICASSO PAINTING IS A BIG STORY! EVERYONE THINKS WE DID IT!

THE POLICE CAME TO OUR HOUSE AND ASKED LOTS OF QUESTIONS. MY DAD WAS REALLY ANGRY WITH ME.

THE COUNCIL CALLED THIS MORNING. THEY'RE NOT GOING TO GIVE US ANY MORE SPRAY-PAINT NOW.

WE CAN'T FINISH THE MURAL WITHOUT THEIR MONEY.

MUCH LATER, THE SPOOKY SKATERS ARRIVED. THEY WANTED TO KNOW MORE ABOUT THE MYSTERY OF THE PAINTING AT THE GALLERY PARTY ...

FOLLOW YOUR NOSES, MY FRIENDS!

MMMM... I SMELL PIZZA!

YUK! IT'S REALLY OLD PIZZA FROM THE FLOOR!

A BIG, HUNGRY DOG'S COMING, JUJU!

HELP!

STOP IT NOW, BOYS...

HEY, I CAN SMELL SOMETHING...

OH NO! NOT MORE PIZZA!

NO. IT'S DIFFERENT... WHAT IS IT?

PABLO WAS TIRED. HIS CLOTHES WERE DIRTY. HE SPOKE WITHOUT A SMILE.

TELL US EVERYTHING. WE'RE LISTENING.

WELL, MANY YEARS AGO, I WAS AN ARTIST. I LIVED IN SPAIN.

SOME OF MY FRIENDS WERE FAMOUS ARTISTS LIKE PICASSO.

NO ONE WANTED TO BUY MY ART.

MY WIFE LEFT ME. MY OLD FRIENDS WENT AWAY TO FRANCE AND AMERICA.

I WAS POOR AND ALONE. NOW NO ONE KNOWS MY WORK OR MY NAME.

THAT'S SO SAD.

THAT'S TERRIBLE.

THANKS TO YOU, THE SKATE KIDS CAN'T SKATE HERE NOW. EVERYONE HATES THEM.

THE POLICE ARE WATCHING THEM.

I'M SORRY. NOW I FEEL TERRIBLE. WHAT CAN I DO TO HELP?

I'VE GOT AN IDEA. WE CAN HELP YOU, BUT YOU MUST STAY IN THE LAND OF THE DEAD AFTER TONIGHT.

YES, OK. THE PICASSO PAINTING IS VERY IMPORTANT. I MADE A STUPID MISTAKE.

YOU CAN STILL CHANGE THINGS. COME ON! LET'S GO!

THE GALLERY WAS CLOSED. IT WAS DARK AND EMPTY.

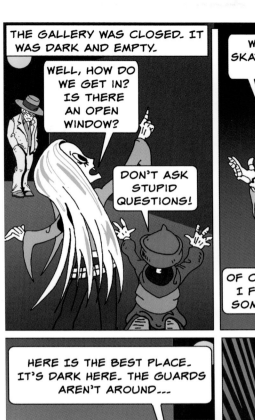

WELL, HOW DO WE GET IN? IS THERE AN OPEN WINDOW?

DON'T ASK STUPID QUESTIONS!

WE'RE THE SPOOKY SKATERS! WE CAN SKATE THROUGH WALLS!

OF COURSE. I FORGET SOMETIMES

HERE IS THE BEST PLACE. IT'S DARK HERE. THE GUARDS AREN'T AROUND...

OK EVERYONE ? FOLLOW ME! COME ON, PABLO! ONE, TWO, THREE...!

PABLO WAS A GREAT PAINTER. THE SPOOKY SKATERS WATCHED HIM FOR HOURS.

HE'S VERY SLOW...

REMEMBER, JUJU, IT'S A VERY SPECIAL PAINTING.

IT'S BORING, ZOMBOY. SHOW ME SOME SKATE STUNTS.

NOT NOW, JUJU. THIS IS AN IMPORTANT JOB.

I'M HUNGRY ...

IT'S TIME FOR ME TO LEAVE NOW. JINX, CAN YOU PAINT THE LAST COLOUR?

OF COURSE. WE HAVE TO LEAVE SOON TOO.

GOODBYE, SPOOKY SKATERS, AND THANK YOU FOR EVERYTHING.

HURRY UP, JINX!

I LOVE THIS COLOUR....

THE NEXT DAY, BACK IN THE LAND OF THE DEAD ---

DO YOU THINK PABLO IS HAPPY HERE NOW?

I HOPE SO- HE'S GOT A NEW HOBBY.

PABLO WAS BUSY AT THE OLD SKATE PARK ---

THIS SAD OLD PLACE IS GOING TO COME ALIVE!

GRAFFITI? TERRIBLE!

FORGET PABLO! I'M STILL BORED! WHO WANTS TO WATCH A SKATE DVD?

I'M STILL CHOOSING PAINT COLOURS- THIS ONE IS SO PRETTY ---

GROAN...

WHEN CAN WE PLAY IN THE LAND OF THE LIVING AGAIN?

SOON - WHEN IT'S DARK.

IN THE LAND OF THE LIVING, ADAM, RICK AND MIA WERE ALMOST FAMOUS! EVERYONE LOVED THEIR MURAL.

WOW! THE NEWSPAPERS AND TV PEOPLE ARE HERE!

YEAH, THEY FILMED ME! I DID A REALLY COOL STUNT!

TURN THIS WAY! LET'S HAVE A PHOTO!

JUST SMILE!

I CAN'T BELIEVE IT!

TELL US ABOUT YOUR FANTASTIC MURAL. WHICH ONE OF YOU IS PABLO?

PABLO? HE'S ...

HE'S NOT HERE. HE STAYS AWAY FROM THE CAMERAS.

BUT WE ALL LOVE HIS WORK. HE'S GREAT!

NOW OUR SUBWAY'S ALIVE WITH SKATING AND PAINTING!

GRAFFITI:

Graffiti on a New York train

OLD GRAFFITI

Graffiti is pictures or words on buildings. Graffiti isn't new. In fact, graffiti started a long time ago! There was graffiti (carvings on walls) in Ancient Greece and Rome.

COOL GRAFFITI

Graffiti artists use spray paint to write their names on walls. This

FAMOUS GRAFFITI ARTISTS

Jean-Michel Basquiat was the first famous street artist. He was from Brooklyn in New York. In 1967, when he was 17, Basquiat and his friend started spray-painting graffiti art around New York. Basquiat's tag was SAMO. Five years later people bought his paintings for millions of dollars.

Jean-Michel Basquiat and one of his paintings

An Os Gemeos painting on the Tate Modern gallery in London

Os Gemeos are brothers. Their names are Otavio and Gustavo Pandolfo and they are from Brazil. They started painting graffiti in 1987. They paint very big yellow people. Their paintings cover many buildings and walls in São Paulo. Their art has something to say about life in Brazil.

ART FROM THE STREET

is 'tagging'. Graffiti was cool in the 70's and 80's. Graffiti artists wanted their 'tags' everywhere. They covered New York City trains in tags.

VANDALISM OR ART?

Some people think that graffiti is vandalism. Others think that it is art – 'street art'. Graffiti is usually illegal but some people are happy to have it on their buildings. Street art is often funny and clever. Today famous art galleries have exhibitions of street art.

> **What do you think?**
> **Is graffiti important?**
> **Is it art or vandalism?**

A Banksy painting on a wall

Banksy is a famous street artist. He comes from Bristol in south-west England and his art is on many buildings around the world. His paintings are often funny and say important things about life.

> **What do these words mean? You can look in a dictionary.**
> carving   illegal   vandalism

Art Galleries
Three of the best!

Art galleries can be exciting places to visit – inside and outside!

Here are three of the best from around the world.

Puppy by Jeff Koons

THE GUGGENHEIM, BILBAO

Q: Where is it?

A: It's next to the River Nervión in Bilbao, Spain.

Q: What does it look like?

A: The building has many curved walls and it looks like a boat.

Q: How old is it?

A: It opened in 1997 and it brings many people to Bilbao.

Q: What can you see there?

A: Outside, people see a sculpture of a dog, twelve metres high, with 40,000 flowers on it!

Q: What do people say about it?

A: "It's the greatest building of our time."

Go to (**www.guggenheim.org**)
Click on **Bilbao**.

THE GUGGENHEIM, NEW YORK

Q: Where is it?

A: It's on Fifth Avenue in New York, near Central Park.

Q: What does it look like?

A: It's easy to find because it looks like a shell.

Q: How old is it?

A: The Guggenheim was fifty years old in 2009. It was the first ever Guggenheim art gallery.

Q: What can you see there?

A: You walk down from the top and see the paintings and sculptures.

Q: What do people say about it?

A: "The outside looks like a car park!"

Go to www.guggenheim.org
Click on **New York**.

The Weather Project by Olafur Eliasson

TATE MODERN, LONDON

Q: Where is it?

A: It's on the south side of the River Thames in London, opposite St Paul's Cathedral.

Q: What does it look like?

A: It's a long brown building.

Q: How old is it?

A: The gallery opened in 2000, but the building is much older.

Q: What can you see there?

A: It's a fantastic gallery to see very big art. One room is 35 metres high and 152 metres long. Many people enjoyed the big yellow sun by Olafur Eliasson.

Q: What do people say about it?

A: "It's a great place to meet."

Go to www.tate.org.uk

Which of these art galleries would you like to go to? Why?

What do these words mean? You can look in a dictionary.
car park   curved   flower   sculpture   shell

Pablo Picasso

Pablo Picasso is one of the world's most important artists. He was alive from 1881 to 1973. He was Spanish, but he lived for a long time in France.

YOUNG ARTIST

Young Pablo always wanted to be an artist. When he was a child he had art lessons from his father, who was also a painter. Then, when he was sixteen, he went to the best art school in Spain.

PARIS – CENTRE OF ART

In 1900 he moved to Paris. It was a very exciting time! Paris was the centre of art in Europe. Pablo Picasso found lots of new friends and learned a new language. At first he was very poor. He burned lots of his paintings to keep his room warm!

RICH AND FAMOUS!

After a few years his life was very different. Some of his paintings were gloomy; paintings of sad women in blue and green paint. Some were happier; paintings in orange and pink of people playing music. People liked his paintings and they bought them. Soon he was rich and famous!

Look at the paintings by Picasso on these pages. Which one do you like most? Why? Work in pairs.

Three Musicians

Guernica

DIFFERENT PAINTINGS

Picasso is most famous for his Cubist work. Cubist paintings looked different from other paintings at the time. The shapes in these pictures look flat. Some of Picasso's Cubist pictures have got bits of newspaper and wallpaper in them. This is 'collage'. Some are about war and have very strong ideas in them, like '*Guernica*' above.

BEING ALONE

When Picasso wasn't painting, he hated being alone. He had many friends and girlfriends. In his life, he married twice and he had four children.

EXPENSIVE!

Picasso was 91 when he died. Most of his work went to the French government who opened a special gallery, the Musée Picasso, in Paris. Now Picasso's paintings are some of the most expensive paintings in the world. Someone bought one painting, 'Garçon à la pipe' for over a hundred million U.S. dollars ($100,000,000) in 2004!

What do these words mean? You can look in a dictionary.

burn   flat   government   gloomy   marry   shape

PAGES 4 – 12

Before you read
Use your dictionary for these questions.

1 Which of the words are linked to **a)** art and **b)** skating?
exhibition   gallery   half-pipe   painting
skater   security guard   stunt   subway

2 Complete the sentences with the words.
art   graffiti   mural   spray-paint
a) … is writing or pictures on walls. People also call graffiti 'street …'.
Street artists often use **c)** … to paint on walls. Councils sometimes ask
graffiti artists to paint a **d)** … on one of their buildings.

3 Match the words to their meanings.
  a) spooky   having nothing to do / not interested
  b) land   frightening
  c) bored   country
  d) closed   not open

4 Where is the ground?
  a) under your feet   **b)** above your head

5 Look at 'People and Places' on pages 4–5. Answer the questions.
  a) What is Jinx's favourite thing?
  b) What are Adam, Rick and Mia's hobbies?
  c) Who has problems?
  d) Why don't the Spooky Skaters like the Land of the Dead?
  e) How do the Spooky Skaters go up to the Land of the Living?
  f) Where do Adam, Rick and Mia like to skate?

After you read

6 Why…
  a) can Rick still paint?
  b) don't some people like the mural?
  c) don't the security guards like Adam, Rick and Mia?
  d) can't Adam, Rick and Mia go into the exhibition?
  e) can't the Spooky Skaters go skating?

f) does Jinx go to Pablo's paint shop?

g) does Mia shout at the man?

7 What do you think the Spooky Skaters are going to do next?

PAGES 12 – 19

Before you read

8 Find the best word for these spaces. Use your dictionary.

artist   ghosts   mystery   forever

1 I love London. I would like to live here …!

2 Who stole the painting? It's a …!

3 I love painting. When I grow up, I would like to be an …

4 Many people don't believe in … but I saw one when I stayed in a castle.

9 Guess the answer to these questions. Then read and check.
The Spooky Skaters see a man painting on the mural. Who is he? What is he going to do?

After you read

10 Put these sentences in the correct order.

a) The police went to Rick's house.

b) Adam, Rick and Mia loved the new graffiti on their mural.

c) Someone painted on a Picasso painting.

d) The security guards ran after the Spooky Skaters.

e) The council said that Adam, Rick and Mia can't have any more spray-paint.

f) The Spooky Skaters found Pablo painting in the subway.

11 Answer these questions.

a) Why doesn't Pablo like his paint shop?

b) What was on TV last night?

c) What does Juju skate on?

12 What do you think?
Why do you think Pablo is painting the mural in the Land of the Living?

PAGES 20 – 25

Before you read

13 Put the letters in the correct order to find a word that means the opposite of *dead*.   leiav ....

14 Guess the answers to the next part of the story. Read and check.
   a) Where did Pablo come from?
   b) What job did he do?
   c) Who was his friend?

After you read

15 Who…
   a) has dirty clothes?
   b) likes black?
   c) laughs about the Picasso painting?
   d) painted on the Picasso painting?

16 What do you think?
   Why did Pablo paint on Picasso's painting?

PAGES 26 – 31

Before you read

17 Guess the answer to the question. Read and check.
   What is the Spooky Skaters' plan?

After you read

18 Read the sentences. Choose the correct words.
   a) The spooky skaters go into the gallery through the *window* / *wall*.
   b) The security guards are *in the gallery* / *at home*.
   c) Pablo painted *quickly* / *slowly*.
   d) Pablo *must* / *mustn't* stay in the Land of the Dead from now.
   e) Pablo finds a new *girlfriend* / *hobby* in the Land of the Dead.
   f) Adam, Nick and Mia *love* / *hate* being famous.

19 What do you think?
   What do Adam, Rick and Mia do next?